INDUSTRIAL SOUTH YORKSHIRE
IN PICTURES

Industrial South Yorkshire in Pictures

PAUL WALTERS & GILES BREARLEY

Wharncliffe Publishing Limited

First Published in 1997 by
Wharncliffe Publishing Limited
an imprint of
Pen and Sword Books Limited,
47 Church Street, Barnsley,
South Yorkshire. S70 2AS

Copyright © Photographs: Paul Walters
Text: Giles Brearley

For up-to-date information on other titles produced under the
Wharncliffe imprint, please telephone or write to:

Wharncliffe Publishing Limited
FREEPOST
47 Church Street
Barnsley
South Yorkshire S70 2BR
Telephone (24 hours): 01226 - 734555

ISBN: 1-871647-43-6

A CIP catalogue record of this book is available from the
British Library

Front cover: A collier at Ticklecock Fair
Conisbrough (49634)
Back cover: Workers at Parkgate carefully
controlling a recently forged ingot. (49648)

Printed in Great Britain by
Redwood Books, Trowbridge, Wiltshire

CONTENTS

An old cottage in Swinton.

INTRODUCTION

MIKE WALTERS was born in January 1933 in Mexborough. At an early age, what was to become a lifelong enthusiasm for photography, was kindled by the fact that his father was a commercial photographer working for the *Daily Mirror*.

Educated at Mexborough Grammar School he then went on to Worksop College. On completion of his course there, he was called up for National Service, during which he rose to the rank of Captain in the Royal Army Ordnance Corps.

In 1955 he left the army and opened the photographic business of M.T. Walters and Associates. He rapidly developed an excellent reputation and his list of commercial clients grew equally swiftly. Much of his early work was done in South Yorkshire., but as his reputation grew he travelled far and wide, visiting Malawi, Trinidad and Tobago, Jamaica, Canada, the United States and numerous European countries.

He developed his own special lighting techniques, which were especially sucessful in capturing the inherent drama of steelmaking. As a result he was regularly commissioned by British Steel and his work appeared in their brochures which were circulated worldwide. In addition he was frequently producing photographs for Hadfields, Simon Carves, Danish Bacon, Kier Construction, The National Coal Board and various Co-operative societies in and around South Yorkshire.

Mike's work received national acclaim when he was presented with the National Architectural Photographic Award., which was made by the British Institute of Professional Photography., in 1986. This award was made for a view of London.

Among the many prestigious assignments which Mike undertook was one with very particular requirements, this was the photographing of the interior of the Reform Club in London. It had the proviso that none of the members present while he was working, would be identifiable in the resulting photographs !

Throughout his life Mike maintained a meticulous archive of his work from his first to his last pictures, leaving a marvellous collection of some 27,000 photographs which only ceased to grow when he was forced to stop work through ill health.

His own interests were centred around the period of the industrial revolution and church architecture. As with his commissioned work, he maintained a meticulous record of his leisure interests, which at the time of his death he was incorporating into a book.

In August 1959 Mike married Pat and they settled in Old Denaby. They had two sons, Paul and Gareth, and as had been the case with his own father, he passed much of his skill and know how on to them. Paul has carried on the family tradition, with his own commercial photographic studio and an international clientele.

Paul feels that the publication of his father's archives will, with it's unique record of industry and working conditions past and present, provoke a flood of memories and an awareness of the changes which have taken place in the towns and countryside of South Yorkshire since the mid-fifties.

Copies of the photographs in this book may be obtained by quoting the number at the end of the picture caption and writing to Paul Walters care of Wharncliffe Publishing Limited, Barnsley.

Figure 1. 15th September 1972. Mexborough Grammar School – English Schoolboys
Winning Team.
Back row: *S. Hollings, R E Bennett, T Slater, K Foster, S Towning, G Snow, D Mullholland,
S Long, D Nichol, G Shield, D Cairns.*
Front row: *T Lines, M Thomas, K Mason, B Burden, M Orgill, P Butterfield* (32560)

Figure 2. 15th January 1970. The new interior of the Yorkshire Bank. Note the complete
absence of security screens and calculators. One large adding machine can be seen
against the back wall. (23643)

Figure 3. 21st July 1963. This fine building was constructed on a site which had previously been a quarry and had later been occupied by a travelling theatre whose company formed the foundation of the Mexborough Hippodrome. The building shown was erected in approximately 1900 and little has changed on it since, with the exception of the arcade at the far left hand end which had been previously used by Jacksons Supermarket. (7054)

Figure 4. 28th March 1968. The refurbished Empress Ballroom at Mexborough. Sadly it seems in recent years, to have lost it's way and at time of going to press it is boarded up. It served the town well for many years and is reputed to have one of the finest sprung ballroom floors in the area.(16406)

Figure 5. 2nd April 1963. A shot of high street Mexborough showing from left to right the facades of Dorothy Leach's shop, she lived in Adwick Road Mexborough. Snelson Electrical Contractors and Benjamin Harold the Jewellers. As you will see a Snelsons rental television in 1963 was 8s.3d (42p), per week for a 19 inch set. A window poster also announces the new 625 line screens. Weekly television rental from 6s.9d (38p) is also advertised. None of these businesses remain. (6888).

Figure 6. 7th December 1971. Since it's construction there has been little outward change to the National Westminster Bank building on Bank Street, Mexborough. Originally built for the Provincial Bank, but following a series of mergers it is now occupied by the National Westminster Bank, who have inherited what must be classed as one of the better buildings in the town.
(31051).

Figure 7. Home Farm Products continued to trade into the 1980s. The notice on the windows extols the virtues of "the finest Ulster Bacon", which was renowned for quality at the time but later fell victim to EEC competition. (10040)

Figure 8. 1st October 1962. Dewhurst the butchers, of 38 High Street, Mexborough.

This shop closed in 1994 after the collapse of the Vestey empire, of which it was a part. Prior to the collapse, Vestey's had operated over 1,000 butcher shops throughout Britain. However the era of the meat kings, like so many other specialist retailers, ceased with the onslaught of the supermarket and yet another High Street tradition was lost.
(7560)

Figure 9. 22 February 1971. This photograph was taken on the day the machinery arrived to commence preparing for the construction of the new Mexborough Sewage Works and shows the greenfield site chosen for this development. This new installation was instigated by Mr Harold Brearley, the then Chief Public Health Inspector, because the existing facilities were not coping with the needs of the expanding housing development on land to the west of Adwick Road, this being the Clayfield and Manor Estates.   (12777)

Figure 10. 10 March 1966. This building was originally constructed for the Savings Bank., which was eventually absorbed into the Midland Bank group. Following the closure of the Midland Bank in these premises, it now houses a bookmakers. The building is particularly fine with some excellent stone carving which enhance it's appearance. It is strongly believed in the area, that Midland Bank were mistaken when they closed the Mexborough branch, leaving them with only one branch in the Dearne Valley. (10017)

Figure 11. 10th June 1965. Photograph of Boots the Chemists, which was in Mexborough well into the 1990s, when the premises were sold to the current occupiers, Lloyds Chemists. The Boots company was formed in Nottingham in late Victorian times and the Mexborough shop was one of many town centre branches operated by them.. (9255a)

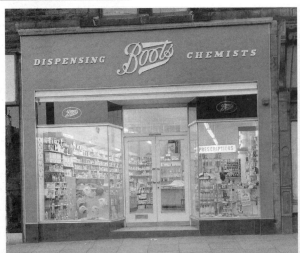

Figure 12. 4th April 1963. This photograph shows Bank Street Mexborough from Number 64 to number 72. These premises have known many changes of owners over the years. The occupiers at time of going to press are. Joanne Prince Beauty Salon, First Call Building Services, Raz-mataz, Fabrics and Dowlings Army Store. Built in the late Victorian era, the properties are well constructed with stone fronts. The shop with the blind outstretched was owned by Graham Oliver's parents. In those days, every Saturday afternoon it was besieged by hundreds of kids who poured out of the Majestic Cinema opposite, following the childrens' matinee film show.   (6899)

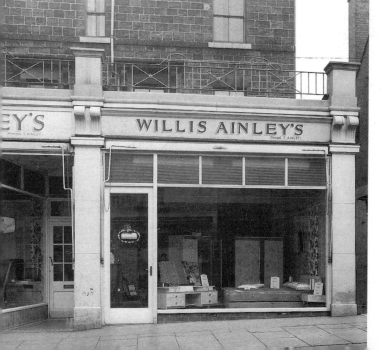

Figure 13. 4th April 1963. This photograph shows two of the properties owned by Willis Ainley's furnishers. Above and behind can be seen two semi-detached houses. In 1970 a youth was arrested at one of these and charged with the murder of a juvenile. The other house was also a murder scene, following a husband and wife dispute. The houses were demolished in the early 1970s. (6898)

Figure 14. 4th April 1963. Photograph showing The Flower Shop., which went on to become Interflora. The Sheffield Telegraph and Star office acted as employer for generations of schoolboys doing newspaper sales and deliveries. Also captured is the corner of Willis Ainley's furniture store which traded for many years in the town. (6897)

Figure 15. 4th April 1963. One of the few known shots of the legendary Whitehouse Café located on High Street. These days, this building seems to conjure up more nostalgic talk among the citizens of Mexborough than any other, no doubt due to its being a popular meeting place in its day. Abutting the building is the Yorkshire Penny Bank of its day, who commissioned this photograph prior to demolition of the café to facilitate the extension of the bank. (6895)

Figure 16. 15th January 1970. The new Yorkshire Bank building on the site previously occupied by the Whitehouse Café. These extended premises are sandwiched between Pettit's shoe shop and the church. Yorkshire Bank are sucessors to the Yorkshire Penny Bank. (23642)

Figure 17. 25th November 1974. The Oriental Chambers on Bank Street were constructed in 1913. and have changed little over the years. The building on the right which briefly housed The Book Corner, was originally part of the Montague Hospital. This building has since been demolished and the Oriental Chambers now stand alone. (36600))

Figure 18. The interior of the Wishing Well Café on High Street, Mexborough, following refurbishment to typical '60s café style. Always a popular venue, the Wishing Well has had a number of owners in it's lifetime. Around the time of this photograph the Wishing Well operated one of very few late licences and hence, there were regular queues for tables on a Saturday night as the pubs were closing. The owner at that time sported an Acker Bilk style beard. He persuaded the Town Council to let him have the only late licence in the town at that time.   (6850)

Figure 19. 4th April 1963. Photograph of High Street, Mexborough, showing L & G Modes of London which operated in town from the 1930s, bringing out-of-date West End fashions to the Mexborough ladies. (69013)

Figures 20 & 21. These two photographs show keen motorsports enthusiasts.
Top photograph: From left to right, Vaughan Midgely, Pat Wagstaff, Bob Wainwright and Dr Barry Ford. *Bottom photograph:* This shows Vaughan Midgely with Dr Barry Ford (in driver's seat). They are trying out a car which Pat Wagstaff was constructing at the time, apparently powered by a Triumph motorcycle engine. The four men were known as the Mexborough Sprint Team.   (9613a & 9613b)

Figure 22. 4th April 1963. This building, standing at the junction of Cliff Street and Glasshouse Lane, was originally part of the offices of Barons Glass Works. Today it is occupied by Constant Security Services Limited. To the side of the building is a board identifying the offices of the ill-fated Mexborough Investments Co., which closed under a cloud in the 1970s. To the far right of the picture is the exterior of Holmes's Pop Factory. These premises are now occupied by Bob Davies's Pladrest Heating Limited. (6893)

Figure 23. 19 January 1962. A shot of a Hamax distribution vehicle. Hamax operated for many years in the Mexborough area as manufacturers of bleaches and disinfectants, latterly producing washing up liquids and household cleaning agents. The company passed from the Hamer family in 1991, but continued trading under the name of South Yorkshire Supplies and Hamax Products until 1994., when it finally closed. (5722)

Figure 24. Photograph of numbers 78 to 80 High Street, Mexborough. The Singer sewing machine shop occupied prominent premises in Mexborough for many years, the manufacture of 'own clothes' and their repair, being an essential part of family life. To the left of the Singer shop is 'Jaquies 40s Dress Shop' which demonstrates the changing times as cheaper imported clothes became generally available. The site of Jaquies 40s Dress Shop was later developed into the Wishing Well Café. To the right of this photograph can be seen the traffic lights which functioned from the mid 1940s to the 1960s, controlling the flow of traffic from Swinton and through the town. Local children took great delight in jumping up and down on the switching strips in the road surface, making the lights change and greatly annoying passing motorists ! (6900)

Figure 25. 11 June 1972. In this photograph Wendy Millington of Modern Foods (Mexborough) Limited, explains the virtues of the product, while practising the art of selling on a potential customer. (C32078

Figure 26. 22 March 1968. The nurses rest room at the Montague Hospital. Examination of the hairstyles shows the varying fashions preferred by different generations. (16325)

Figure 27. 31 January 1977. This photograph shows the tea bar of Mexborough Hospital which was refurbished by public fundraising, a great achievement at the time. Much of the fundraising work was carried out by Vera Styling and her husband George, known as "The Colonel". They lived in Mexborough and were well known for their charitable and fundraising activities. (39194

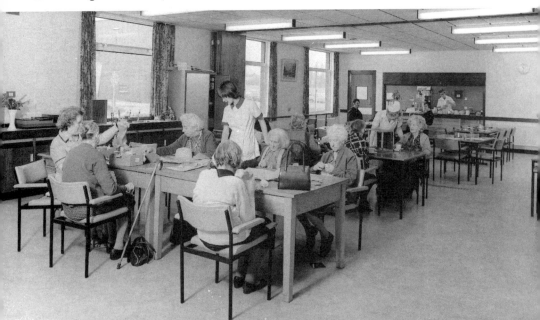

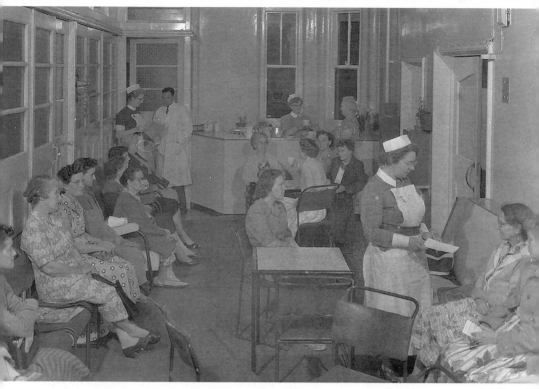

Figure 28. 11th September 1959. The outpatients waiting room of Montague Hospital. Founded in 1889 after a campaign led by Dr Sykes and Andrew Montague of Melton Hall. In recognition of the enormous contribution to the cause of the hospital made by Mr Montague, it carried his name. (3774) (3730-33)

Figure 29 1st September 1959. Anyone for a leg off ? The mens surgical ward of Montague Hospital. (3731)

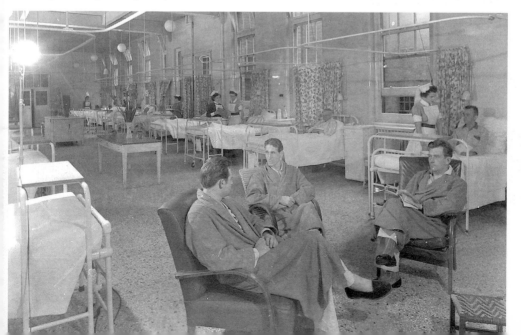

Figure 30. 1969. Local personalities of the day. *Back row left to right:* Doug Snape, Jack Spencer, Lilian Spencer, Tom Squires and Harry Sale. *Front row seated:* Phillis Snape, Madge Squires, The Chief Rabbi of Sheffield, Tom Walters, Mabel Walters, Cath Sayle. (49635)

Figure 31. 29th May 1970. An election campaign photograph of Brian O'Malley. Brian was the Don Valley Labour M.P. until 1976, when he tragically died whilst delivering a speech. His death was a sad loss to the community. He was elected as the member for Don Valley on the 3rd of April 1963, appointed Chief Whip in 1964, Minister of State to the DHSS in 1974 and was made a Privy Councillor in 1975. (25129)

Figure 32. 4th November 1968. This photograph shows Jack Watson, landlord of the Bulls Head on High Street, christening the new bar. Jack's son, also called Jack, later took a pub of his own at Scarborough. (19527)

Figure 33. 6th March 1963. An apprentice representing Modern Meat Marketing Limited, being adjudged at the semi-finals of the Meat Presentation Contest, hosted by Barnsley Co-op. (6855)

Figure 34. 11th June 1975. This photograph shows the newly constructed Bowbroom bridge, from which many suicides have taken place since it's opening. Passing under the bridge is an English Electric type 3 diesel locomotive travelling towards Wath. (37300)

Figure 35. 11th June 1973. A Modern Foods Limited van being loaded for yet another delivery. (C32073)

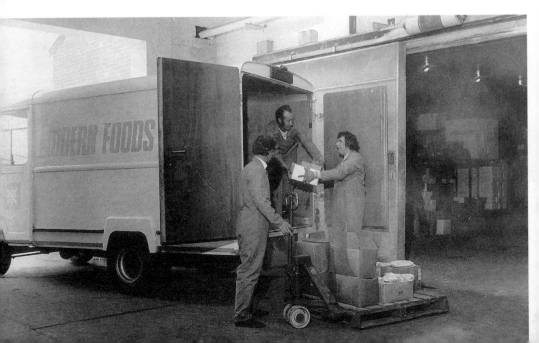

Figure 36. 11th June 1973. Keep your coats on lads! Stock being checked inside the big freezer room at Modern Foods Ltd.

Figure 37. 20th May 1970. This photograph of the Mexborough bypass development shows to the right, stone cottages which have since been demolished. The cottages, thought to have been built in the early 1800s where covered in ivy at the front. Fennell Construction Limited have since built a block of flats on the site. (25084)

Figure 38. 25th February 1959. An exterior photograph of Clays Television Repair Depot. The depot was located in Leach Lane alongside the canal. At that time, Clays vans were a familiar sight around the town. (3352)

Figure 39 26th February 1959. An interior photograph of Clay's repair workroom, showing the staff in action. (3353)

Figure 40. 24th April 1961. The transport fleet of Holmes Pop Factory outside it's Cliff Street premises and promising good health to all who indulged! The park at the rear of the factory was very popular with children, due to the possibility of cadging free pop from the staff. Or even helping themselves after dark! These nocturnal visits being in part deterred by a female police officer nicknamed "Rubber Lips", who fortunately for the kids, was none too nimble. Following Mr Holmes's death, his widow who had been my father's secretary, sought a new life in Australia. (4893)

Figure: 41. 6th May 1960. Photograph of Pettits Shoe Shop in High Street, with a glimpse of the Rediffusion shop on the right. (4220)

Figure 42. 14th March 1960. Photograph of Ben Bailey on site, checking the progress of the latest construction project. (4069)

Figure 43. The Primitive Methodist Sunday School building before Mike Walters turned it into his photographic studio. Today the building houses the studio of Worldwide Photography and is shared by the South Yorkshire Times and Haworth Graphics. (49636)

Figure 44. 20th June 1961. A view of the ingot ring jig plant of Robert Bowram & Co Ltd, part of London & Scandinavian Metallurgical Ltd. It is believed that this plant was situated in the Cliff Street area of the town. (5042)

Figure 45. 30th November 1960. The Yorkshire Region Controller of the CEGB carrying out his own tour of inspection of Mexborough power station. (4623C)

Figure 46. 1st December 1960. Students from Schofield Technical School, Mexborough, during a tour of the power station. The power station was built on land originally allocated for alloments, before it's purchase from Mexborough Council in 1940. (4624)

Figure 47. 22nd April 1963. The congregation of the Wesleyan Church in their Sunday best. (6924)

Figure 48. 11th August 1960. This shot was not taken by Mike Walters, but by one of his staff. It is of his and his new wife Pat's wedding party. Following the wedding ceremony a number of photographs were taken around the ferry boat slipway. (49637)

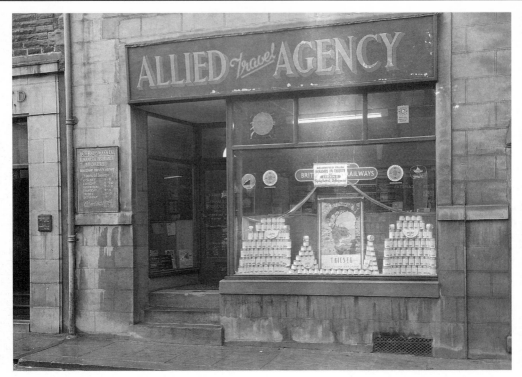

Figure 49. 10th November 1960. The Main Street frontage of Allied Travel Agency, with Bourne and Swan to the left. A promotion involving travel aided by Heinz baked beans is featured in Allied's window ! (4577)

Figure 50. 5th December 1961. The Caravan Site on Church Street. Following pressure by Harold Brearley, Chief Public Health Inspector, the site owners tidied it up and provided facilities in line with new Public Health Laws. The site still operates today, but is hardly recognisable from the above state, with landscaping and private facilities. (5613)

Figure 51. 8th January 1963. The newly constructed Co-operative store at Cedar Avenue. In the 1960s the Barnsley co-operative were embarking on a programme of expansion and modernisation of their stores. Moving away from the traditional and towards self-service stores. The land upon which the Highwoods estate stands, was bought from Manvers Main Colliery Company by the Town Council in 1940. The first Co-operative store opened in Mexborough in 1880. (6784)

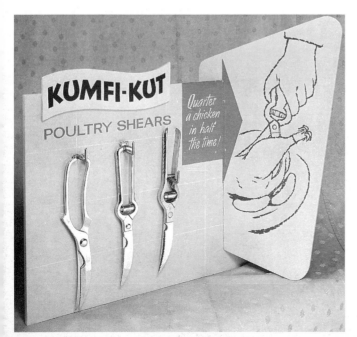

Figure 52. 7th January 1963. A promotional photograph for Champion Scissors, who traded from premises in Cliff Street for many years. The premises were later occupied by an engineering and engine rebuilding company. (6778)

Figure 53. 23rd October 1959. The Holmes and Son promotional road show kicked off at the Empire Cinema. Exactly what "syncopating Sandy" actually did is not recorded, but we can safely assume it was an effervescent performance ! (J3874)

Figure 54. 2nd December 1961. Not to be outdone, Coca Cola launched a promotion at the Empress Ballroom. At that time the American company was pushing hard for a larger market share, with a whole series of promotional road shows. (5608)

Figure 55. 2nd December 1957. Frank Walters began his professional life selling oranges outside the Hippodrome in Mexborough before setting up the Walters removal business. By the 1950s, Frank owned a fleet of four removal vans, with a yard and specially adapted garages on Victoria Road. This new van was photographed not long before the company was sold to the Barnsley Co-operative Society. Frank was employed by the Co-op until 1961, when he bought a post office and shop in North Yorkshire. The shot was taken on Harlington Lane with the junction of Tennyson Avenue. (2443 and 2445)

Figure 56. 29th April 1968. Coal barges undergoing repairs at Waddingtons boat yard. (16871)

Figure 57. 5th September 1960. Operating the Plant at Ward and Sons (Swinton) Limited. The factory was situated at the junction of Bridge Street and Rowms Lane. The factory was built on the site of an historic market and partly on the site of the Don Pottery. Wards was later taken over by Bass Charrington and was finally closed. The buildings were then taken over by Housecraft as a builders' merchants which is operated as Shipley's today. (4488 and 4459)

Figure 58. 1st June 1962. The electric iron assembly shop at the GEC factory. Electric irons have been manufactured at this plant since the Second World War. In the early 1960s there was a great shortage of labour in the region, resulting in mass immigration from the West Indies. Some of these immigrant workers seem to have preferred making irons to making steel ! (6451)

Figure 59. 3rd May 1963. The cooker and refrigerator final assembly area at the GEC plant, with the refrigerator line in the foreground. There were day and late evening shifts in operation at this plant. (6936)

Figure 60. 2nd April 1959. Alderman M. Creighton posing for a bust of himself. His family were associated with Swinton Common since 1862, when they lived in a cottage adjoining the woods at Warren Vale Road. Subsequently the woods were named after his family. Alderman Creighton followed in his father's footsteps in public service. His father was a County Councillor. (3427)

Figure 61. View of Queen Street, before development of the estate at the lower end. (2068)

Figure 62. 3rd December 1967. Photograph of Doug Cavill, who at the time operated the Swinton Old Hall Service Station. In later years he became a driving instructor. A local history enthusiast, he has done considerable research into the history of the Rockingham Potteries, and has written histories of the potteries.   (14919)

Figure 63. 30th July 1963. One of the fleet of Austin lorries operated by the General Electric Company. These constantly shuttled back and forth, bringing in components and taking out finished goods. (7110)

Figure 64. 28th May 1963. The newly constructed Cresswell Estate at Swinton showing Queens Avenue. These properties were constructed by Ben Bailey and were the first of the larger semi-detached properties built in the area. (6891)

Figure 65. 19th August 1971. The National Westminster Bank building at the junction of Midland Road and Station Street. Outwardly the building has changed little other than that the building is now covered in rendering. When originally built for the Sheffield Bank, it occupied only the corner property, but expanded into adjoining buildings as banking became more popular. (30178)

Figure 66 and 67. 8th April 1960. Internal and external views of the new Swinton Miners Welfare Club. Sadly the club has now closed. (4132 & 4133)

Figure 68. 26th September 1963. The legendary Roxy cinema in Swinton, a focal point for generations of picture goers. The film being advertised is "The Mind Benders", starring Dirk Bogard. The proprietors at the time of this photograph were Thomas Wade & Sons of Wath-on-Dearne and the Manager was George Whitfield. The cost of admission at the time was: pit 4d., stalls 6d and the circle was 1s. Wade & Sons were also attributed with building the Majestic at Wath-on-Dearne and the Rock at Cudworth. The Roxy now operates as a Sports and Social Club. (7256)

Figure 69. 29th April 1968. A new lock under construction at the canal side. The scene is one of apparent devastation, sadly little has changed to the present day. (16871)

Figure 70 and 71. 8th January 1964. Two photographs of Mrs Pat Walters' car being retrieved from the canal after she had crashed through the bridge opposite the Commercial Inn. Fortunately she was unhurt as the convertible top was open, enabling her to escape and swim to safety. The scene of the accident was attended by Mr Victor Waddington, Chairman of Waddingtons one of the oldest companies in South Yorkshire who, having ensured that Mrs Walters was safe, asked her if she would in future keep her car out of the canal, when he would keep his barges off the roads! Some of Mike's flash bulbs are floating around the car as it is hauled out. In the lower photograph, the bus in the background carries an advert for Snelsons at Mexborough. (49638 & 49639)

Figure 72 and 72. 4th December 1961. Internal and external views of Kilnhurst, the old folks' centre after it's official opening. (5609)

Figure 73. 14th June 1956. Carlyle Street with terraced houses on one side whilst the new Danish Bacon Depot is being built in the forefront. The houses have since been demolished and the ground is now part off the Lime Grove Estate. (1608)

Figure 74. 14th May 1956. Looking down Carlyle Street before the contractors have moved in to begin work on the Danish Bacon Depot. (1539)

Figure 75. 24th August 1961. Management and Sales Force of the Danish Bacon Company, pose for Mike's lens in their brand new offices. (5275)

Figure 76. 24th August 1961. The loading bay of the Danish Bacon Company, clearly demonstrating that the company had not only bacon to bring home ! Boxes containing cooking fat, soap powder, lard, soup, spaghetti and corn flakes are clearly visible. (49639)

Figure 77. The Company commissioned this picture to build into a series depicting the journey of their product from Denmark. Here a crate is being off-loaded at Immingham docks. (49640)

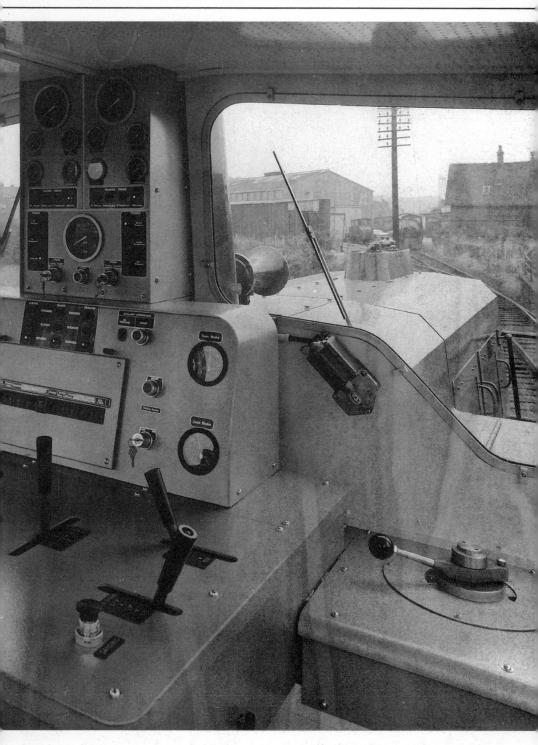

Figure 78. 29th August 1972. A photograph taken from inside the cab of a newly constructed engine, showing the track linking Thomas Hill's locomotive assembly Depot with the main line. (32477))

Figure 79. Locomotives being assembled at Thomas Hill's Depot. The company made numerous locomotives for the National Coal Board as well as other large industrial customers at home and abroad. Sadly the plant closed in the early 1990s.

Figure 80 and 81. 28th February 1973 and 28th March 1967. Two brand new locomotives awaiting delivery to customers.   (33293 & 11833)

Figure 82. 6th November 1957. Sandra Lindsey and June Norman take a break from manufacturing mining detonators at the ICI plant in Denaby. During the Second World War the factory produced military detonators. Once married, girls were only allowed to work on the detonator line for six months, due to the effects of sulphur. Other well known faces are Brenda David, Brenda Tingle, Dot Webster, Rita Bulcraft, Sandra Duke, Doreen Hartley, Maureen Parnham, Irene Taylor, Jean and Margo Rogers. This plant eventually closed in 1964. (2407)

Figure 83. 21st August 1962. Seven men of the ICI Powder Works pose before the Safety League board. The site of the factory was originally chosen for it's isolation, due to the dangerous nature of the work carried out there. The Powder Works closed in the mid 1960s after 70 years of continuous explosives manufacture. (6413)

Figure 84. 21st August 1962. The ladies of the ICI factory in a more formal pose. The mixture of headscarves and the hairstyles of the day present an interesting variety. (6414)

Figure 85. 11th April 1962. An "action shot" of two ladies assembling Detonator wire at ICI. (6009))

Figure 86. 15th October 1961. The Old Denaby Pipe Wrapping Plant of William Press & Sons Ltd, under construction. The skyline of Mexborough can be seen in the far distance over the meadows of Old Denaby. This building is now quite unrecognisable. (5424b. (5424b)

Figure 87. 4th July 1963. A picture designed and taken by Mike at Old Denaby for media design promotion for a customer. The fateful car of Mrs Walters which ended up in the canal at Kilnhurst can be seen in the background.

Figure 88. 1st August 1961. A photograph taken in Mike's home at Old Denaby, with his wife Pat and her friend, a professional model. They are posing before a Baxi fireplace. The photograph was commissioned after Mike had one installed in his property. (5195).

Figure 89. 2nd May 1961. Nuns at the Convent of Sisters of Mercy which was found-ed in Denaby in June of 1927. The nuns quietly went about their work of teaching and administering to the sick and needy in the Denaby Parish over the years. Some of the nuns were trained teachers and assisted in the education of the children. (49641)

Figure 90. A view of Barnburgh Street at Denaby showing the architectural backbone of the township of Denaby as construct-ed in 1898 for the mine workers and their families. The census of 1861 had only 203 people but by 1871 this had risen to 695 and up to 1632 by 1881. Most of the houses were built by Saul and Mitchell from Mexborough. The streets were demolished in 1967. The houses consisted of two rooms plus an attic upstairs, two rooms downstairs and a small back yard, outside toilets and coalplaces. Water was not installed until 1902. Gas from the colliery powered the houses until 1951 when electricity was installed. (49642)

Figure 91. 2 July 1955. The newly constructed Manvers Coal Washery Plant showing the coal preparation ovens and condensors with pit headgear in the background. The plant was constructed by Simon Carves Limited. ((172)

Figure 92. 2 August 1956. The Washery's main conveyor nearing completion. In the distance loaded coal wagons can be seen awaiting servicing. The hills of High Melton, Barnburgh and Hickleton are discernible through the girder work.

Figure 93. 1967. The pupils of Pope Pius School sit in assembly for Mass. The younger girls are wearing the traditional berets, while the older girls sit at the back with appropriate head covering. Spot the one rebellious exception ! (C49641)

Figure 94. 9 April 1969. General view of the High Street taken for Plastic Industrialised Houses Limited, who were considering a project in the area. Little has changed, other than the flow of traffic. ((20989)

Figure 95. 10 July 1969. Picture commissioned by Wilson and Wormsley, toy shop, to show the cracks caused to the building due to subsidence. May Taylor was a trader in Wath for many years, as was Blaskey's bicycle shop. (22002)

Figure 96.   21 January 1969.   Picture commissioned by Bramall and Ogden for a brochure; Peter Copley (foreground) and David Cliffe (kneeling) are putting the finishing touches to an order for church pews. Such was the standard of workmanship that the firm received a National Accolade for their work. The Company ceased trading on the death of Mr Ogden and was taken over by Terry Bramall and later by Tony Jones of Mexborough. It was affected by the recession and stopped trading in the 80s. The site has since been cleared and has recently been redeveloped for housing. (3631)

Figure 97 and 98. 17 October 1973. Well Griffiths Limited operated at Common Road, Wath, for a short while. It remains something of a mystery as to exactly what they did manufacture! (35311) (34414)

Figure 99. 23rd August 1963. This was the new site acquired for the national Provincial Bank. The site is on the corner of Edna Street and Furlong Road. To the right hand side of the photograph can be seen the advertising board of Allatt & Spencer, who are unfortunately no longer trading.   (7163)

Figure 100. 17th February 1963. Phillipsons Coaches line up with pride for this fleet picture. Phillipsons operated for many years out of Goldthorpe carrying generations of local travellers to coast and country, as well as operating regular local services. The company ceased trading in the 1970s. (6835)

Figure 101. 3rd February 1961. The shop parade on Doncaster Road has changed little, apart from these shops in its midst. Of the ones depicted, i.e. Eaton the Chemists, G Wallpapers, Dewhursts, Woolworths etc. none remain. This block was constructed in 1960 by a Bradford Company, H Wood Limited and shows the change in architectural style. (4746)

Figures 102, and 103. 23rd July 1960. As the whole mode of shopping changed, there became a rush on the High Street to create self-service store. Carline's Cash 'n Carry was no exception to this fashion and was established in 1960. The prices depicted, show the vast difference between prices of yester-year and today, as well as how once familiar names have become mere memories. Although Carline's did initially prosper in Goldthorpe, its future was short lived. (4404 and 4405)

Figure 104 and 105. 11th September 1961. The Gas Board was always in competition with the locally dominated coal and electricity supplies. Road Shows were mounted and new uses for gas demonstrated. This shot shows the new concept of a gas fridge, as opposed to traditional refrigeration equipment. This mobile exhibition was photographed in Goldthorpe. (5327)

Figures 106 and 107. 14th July 1960. The sound of saws and cutters operating in the premises of the Goldthorpe Timber Company, echoed across the Furlong Road area of Bolton for many years. The above photograph shows the substantial stocks held and distributed by the company. The lower photograph shows the workforce assembled just before setting off on a social outing. (4376 & 4377)

Figures 108 and 109. 25th January 1959. Co-operative branch no 74 at Bolton-on-Dearne, following its conversion to a self-service store. To the right can be seen the drapery department, while the long serving Horlicks signs still adorn the windows even after the major refit. When first opened in the 1880s, it occupied only the pent roofed building to the right, the adjoining houses being acquired as the business expanded. One of the first managers of this branch was a Mr Robinson.   (3323 & 3324)

Figure 110. 5th May 1961. Excellent photograph showing R Colin Snow's fine vehicle parked at the Barnburgh Colliery Weigh Bridge with the pit head gears in the background. The site has now been fully cleared and nothing remains of this once industrious operation. Snow's now operate a large plant at the Pastures in Mexborough. The colliery was originally sunk in 1912. (4917)

Figure 111. 31st March 1967. An interesting shot showing the M1 reaching Tankersley and Hoyland. The mammoth task of the construction of the M1 was the largest road building project undertaken in Great Britain. The contractors excelled themselves in reaching Tankersley early and the cleared ground stood a while until the roadlayers caught up. The earth moving contractor in the shot is Dowsett Engineering Construction Limited. (18651)

Figure 112. 24th November 1956. Photograph of Mitchell Main Colliery Coal Preparation Area. This colliery was the scene of violence in 1893 when troops had to be drafted in following a pit lock-out. The large crowd met at Mitchells Main, gathering on the canal bridge and the deputies who were leaving the colliery were badly jostled. It was rumoured that strike breakers were working inside the mine. (1920)

Figure 113. 24th November 1956. Further photograph of Mitchell Main colliery, showing surface workers in action loading coal. (1920)

Figure 114. 2nd February 1962. External photograph of Mackridge the Ironmonger's premises, showing this fine building which was constructed in 1891. (5856)

Figure 115. 23rd March 1972. Interior photograph of the Yorkshire Bank following it's second refurbishment to be recorded by Mike's camera. It was obviously a good job as little has changed to the present day, apart from the amounts of money passing through. It is interesting to compare this photograph with that on page 8, particularly the new security screens. (31677)

Figure 116. 8th January 1961. Wombwell Operatic Society after their last performance of Carousel. (4678)

Figure 117. 24th April 1963. Workers engaged in another casting at Wombwell Foundry. (6931)

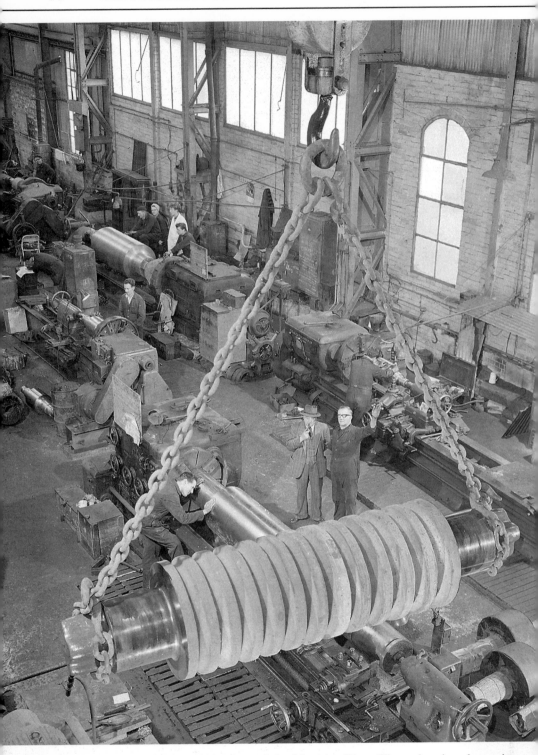

Figure 118. 24th April 1963. Aerial shot of the Machine Shop Floor showing the various milling equipment and lathes utilised. (6927)

Figure 119. At a meeting of the Board of Directors of Barnsley British Co-operative, note the magnificent oak boardroom table. You will observe the company secretary sitting at his own desk in front of the company chairman. (49643)

Figure 120. Barnsley British Co-operative premises on Wellington Street.

Figure 121, 122. 11th May 1961. Barnsley Co-operative Mens Central Tailoring Department. The external shot shows the ongoing modernisation of the Co-operative and an internal (*opposite top right*) shot depicting the wide range of goods and a move towards self-service as much as practical. (4483 and 4487)

Figure 123. The new Grocery Department at the top of Market Street.

Figures 124 and 125. 11 December 1956. The Central Drapery building, known as Island Corner, showing the detailed cast iron curtain walling. The building is now used as a night club. *Below:* Interior of the Drapery Department.

Figure 126. 11 December 1956. Co-operative Phamaceutical Department.
The photographs on these pages are of the co-operative store in Barnsley prior to the
modernisations of the early 1960s.

Figure 127. The Arcadian Restaurant prior to modernisation, showing the art deco style which had clearly lingered too long. (49642)

Figure 128. 12 April 1960. External view of the Birch Avenue Co-operative store. Note the cigarette machines outside the store. These used to be a common sight, sadly today their tamper free life expectancy would be brief indeed. (4138)

Figure 129. 12th April 1960. Internal view of the Co-operative store at Stairfoot. In 1902, the manageress of this store was a Mrs Ambler, the only manageress in the whole of the co-operative society. (4136)

Figure 130 4th December 1961. A Danish Bacon Company van delivering to the butchery traders at Barnsley market. (5609)

Figure 131. 10th June 1969. A view of the newly constructed Arndale Centre. The board announces Heeley and Baker as the letting agents for the centre. This was one of the first purpose built shopping centres in South Yorkshire and it quickly filled up with traders. (22062)

Figure 132. 11th June 1959. Locomotive repairs being carried out at the Plant Works. Doncaster has been linked with the railway industry since the 1840s, with local manufacture and repair operations being carried out on the Plant Works site for many years. (3607)

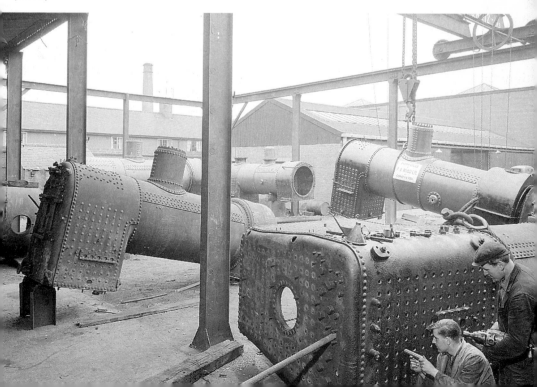

Figure 133. 10th June 1969. A shot showing the alternate entrance to the Arndale Centre. Most of the shops that flanked the front are no longer trading, with the exception of Stead and Simpson. (21680)

Figure 134 February 1974. Internal shot showing the incredible statues that were criticised for being risqué by many of the Doncaster townsfolk. The floor has been taken over by the Scottish Tourist Board in an attempt to persuade South Yorkshire people to holiday in the North. British Home Stores and Boots still occupy the same site as when the centre opened. (33242)

PARKGATE IRON AND STEELWORKS was established by two Sheffield men, Sanderson and Watson in the first quarter of the nineteenth century. The location for the plant was chosen due to the closeness to the canal and the proximity of the coal mines.

Production commenced in 1823 with a small plant manufacturing wrought iron bars and tin plate. In 1832 the name of the company was Birmingham Tin Plate Company. The first blast furnace was installed in 1839. In 1840 William Scholfield became the owner of the business in partnership with Charles Geach and Samuel Beal. In 1854 the company was renamed Samuel Beal and Company. In 1856 the first iron armour plates for warships were manufactured. In 1864 Samuel Beal retired and sold the works to the Parkgate Iron Co. Limited.

In 1888 expansion took place when the billet mill, slab mill and large plate mill were installed and the name of the company was changed to Parkgate Iron and Steel Co. Limited.

In 1956 the company was sold to Tube Investments Limited and a wire department was installed. The site was eventually closed in 1974.

Figure 135. 19th April 1964. Withdrawing molten iron from the 800 ton capacity mixer furnace with the foreman directing the operation. (7940)

Figure 136. 19th April 1964. Tapping of steel from the Kaldo unit into ladled transportation tubs. (49647)

Figure 137. 19th April 1964. Taking the temperature of the steel by immersion pyrometer. (49646)

Figure 138. 1964. The computer room at Parkgate Iron and Steelworks, where the staff are busily engaged in putting information on punched cards. The desk top computer of today is more powerful than the entire computing system these girls are operating. (49649)

Figure 139. 1st November 1972. Miss Great Britain signing autographs for admirers while carrying out promotion work for Lux Soap Products. Note the platform shoes and the style of dress which epitomises the early 1970s. (32741)

Figure 140. 17th November 1966. Renovation work being undertaken on Rotherham power station. The station was shut down and completely demolished in the early 1970s as more efficient stations came on stream. The contractor here is GKN Building Services Ltd. (10755)

Figure 134. 25 October 1974. Grattans new office and distribution block was one of the first projects to re-enhance the town centre of Rotherham. The company operated from these premises until the late 1930s when ownership then reverted to the Council. You will note the Cooling Towers of the Power Station in the background, although by this time it had ceased operation. (C36405)

Figure 142. 1st June 1970. Children enjoying recreation time at Bestwood School. The school had only recently been constructed and was on the lines of all schools built after 1960 which said they, must build flat roofs and use planking for ballustrades. (25142)

Figure 143. 21st May 1963. Taken at Green and Sons Limited. This promotional photograph epitomises the old fashioned British Engineer with a no nonsense steady approach. (49650)

Figure 144. 30th November 1961. Progress photograph of the re-development of property at Moorgate for Pearl Assurance by Wade Construction Co. Limited. To the right hand side can be seen the still existing premises of Merryweather and Corbett, the Estate Agents. (5595)

Figure 145. 21st May 1963. Further shot taken inside the workshop at Green and Sons. The company does not trade today. (6963)

Figure 146. 7th June 1972. The town's answer to housing shortage, which managed to clear slums and create new ones stacked on top of each other, with a higher density to the acre. The Oak Hill Housing Development was designed by G Keenson Barnett and partners to the demands of the 70s. (32063)

Figure 147. 5th April 1960. Photograph taken on Wellgate showing the re-development of a fine Victorian building. Unfortunately, none of the shops shown remain today. It is interesting to note how consumer trends change, in particular with reference to the dyeing service which is now virtually non existent with the higher spending power of the consumer, who does not find it necessary to re-cycle clothes also with fur shop, which would today be seen as controversial. (4125)

Figure 148. 20th December 1972. Construction under way at the Herringthorpe Leisure Centre. It is obviously at an early stage and well before "Mr Brittas" took control. Rotherham Council were quite innovative in the design and structure. (32933)

Figure 149. 23rd August 1973. The newly constructed car park and bus station opposite the Grattan building, was innovative for Rotherham at the time. This building has now been extended and revamped. It was a more acceptable form of the town centre monstrosities in this era. The project was undertaken by John Mowlem & Company. (34277)

Figure 150. 30th September 1960. The famous Steel Peech & Tozer Bridge at Templeborough which added magnitude to Rotherham's steel making operations. The company had operated on this site for many years. The Phoenix Besseman Steel Company went bankrupt and was taken over by Steel Tozer and Hampton in 1875. The company then reformed as Steel Peech & Tozer in 1883 and the Templeborough Melting Shop was established in 1917, housing fourteen 60 ton open hearth furnaces. The building had caused some contention, as it was on the site of Roman fortifications. During 1960 to 1965 the whole company was modernised and the largest electric arc melting shop in the world was created, with six 110 ton furnaces. The Mill closed in 1994 after Steel Peech and Tozer had been taken over. (4477)

Paul Walters began his professional career as a photographer in 1987 when he joined his father's company at the age of 24. His first task in learning his trade, was to assist Michael on a ten country tour of Europe for a multi-national company. It was this marathon ten thousand mile race around the continent that moulded the direction of Paul's career.

Initially working with his father covering major building projects in addition to publications such as the APA guide to Athens, Michael managed to teach Paul not only the practical basics, but how to approach a subject to bring out its best characteristics. They worked together until he was forced into early retirement due to ill health. Michael would use people to bring a subject to life and this is a technique Paul still uses in his work today.

Paul now spends much of his time overseas working for major travel companies, producing photographs for holiday brochures in addition to his UK based work in the production of pictures and exhibitions for Industry and Commerce.

Giles Brearley is a Chartered Management Accountant in practice in Swinton. He was born at Barnsley, but resided at Mexborough. He went to college at High Melton, Doncaster, Sheffield and York. His father was Chief Public Health Inspector for Mexborough from 1940 until 1974. Giles has written other local history books – *Mexborough A Town At War* and *We Will Remember*, (jointly with Graham Oliver) and also wrote *History of Lead Mining in the Peak District* which was based on his years potholing in Derbyshire as a student.